Who's Who
Champions

Compiled by Donna Bailey
Illustrated by Peter Rutherford

HENDERSON
P U B L I S H I N G   P L C

Woodbridge, Suffolk, IP12 1BY England
© 1994 Henderson Publishing plc

A

ADAMSON, *George (1906-1989)*
English naturalist and conservationist

Adamson was a game warden in Kenya in 1938, who became famous when his wife Joy wrote a book, *Born Free* about a lioness called Elsa that they brought up and released into the wild. Joy was murdered in Kenya but George continued their work. He set up a sanctuary where animals could live in freedom, and helped lions return to the wild. A week before he was killed by bandits, his sanctuary was made into a National Park.

ANDERSON, *Elizabeth Garret (1836-1917)*
First qualified English female doctor
Anderson wanted to be a doctor but in those days women were not allowed to practise medicine, so she obtained a diploma from the Society of Apothecaries. She opened a dispensary in a London hospital for poor women. She became the Mayor of Aldeburgh in Suffolk, the first woman mayor in Britain.

AQUINAS, *Saint Thomas (c.1225-1274) Italian scholar*
Thomas wanted to enter the Dominican order of friars, but his family did not want him to become a friar, so his brothers captured him and kept him a prisoner. Thomas finally escaped and went to study religion at university. He became a teacher of philosophy and religion and wrote many books. His comments on the Bible influenced Catholic thought for years to come.

ARISTOTLE, *(384-322 BC) Greek philosopher*
Aristotle was tutor to Alexander the Great, then
opened his own school of philosophy in Athens.
He wrote many books, and his ideas gave rise to the
science of logic, or rules of reasoning, which still has
an effect on how scholars think today.

AUGUSTINE OF HIPPO, *Saint, (354-430)*
Early Christian writer
Augustine was born in Algeria. He was a very
naughty child and continued his wild ways when he
went to university, but was also a brilliant student.
He became a teacher in Italy . One day he decided to
devote his life to God. He returned to Algeria and
became a bishop, and spent much of his time
writing. His teachings have had an important
influence on Christian thinking.

BACON, *Francis (1561-1625)*
English politician and writer

Bacon was a brilliant scholar who tried to encourage people to think on new lines when interpreting science, and to explore new ideas. He is famous for his essays on the men and customs of the age, and his books on philosophy and science.

BADEN-POWELL, *Lord Robert (1857-1941)*
Founder of the Boy Scouts

As a schoolboy, Baden-Powell enjoyed the outdoor life, particularly camping and tracking. He joined the army and was shocked to find how little young men knew about looking after themselves in the open. He was so good at scouting that his enemies called him 'The wolf that never sleeps'. Back in Britain he rewrote his book about scouting as a book for boys, and founded the Boy Scout Movement with the motto 'Be Prepared', from his initials.

BADER, *Sir Douglas (1910-1982)*
British fighter pilot
Douglas Bader lost both his legs in a flying accident in 1931, but he still managed to have a brilliant career as a fighter pilot in World War II. After the war he was knighted for his work with disabled people who were encouraged by his brave example.

BARNARDO, *Dr. Thomas (1845-1905)*
British philanthropist
Barnardo was deeply moved by the hungry, dirty and ragged children he saw in the east end of London, and opened a "ragged school" for them in a donkey stable. Barnardo tracked down homeless children and raised money to provide them with a home and some training. By the time he died, he had helped 60,000 needy children.

BERNARD, *Saint (d.1081?) Italian saint*

When Bernard was in charge of the Aosta diocese in north Italy, he was worried about the travellers crossing the high Alpine passes in the winter. He established two rest houses at the summits of the passes, named the Great St Bernard and the Little St Bernard after him, and trained dogs to find the travellers lost in the snow. These dogs were called St Bernards.

BESANT, *Annie (1847-1933) English social reformer*

Annie Besant, a journalist, campaigned for women's rights and birth control for the women who lived in poverty caring for large families. She supported the strike for better pay by London's 'match girls' who worked 14 hours a day in terrible unhealthy conditions.

BEVERIDGE, *William (1879-1963)*
English social reformer
Beveridge was a social worker in London who
drew up the blueprint for Britain's welfare state.
He believed that unemployment was caused by the
way industry was organised. During World War II
he made a plan to try and solve post-war poverty.
He proposed a social insurance programme
covering illness, unemployment, old age and death.

BOLIVAR, *Simon (1738-18230)*
South American patriot
Bolivar wanted to help free the people of Venezuela
from the rule of the Spanish. He joined a group of
rebels who captured Caracas, the capital of
Venezuela. Bolivar was given the title of The
Liberator. He dreamed of freeing the whole of South
America, and helped defeat Spanish armies in
Ecuador, Peru and Venezuela.

BOOTH, *William (1829-1912)*
Founder of the Salvation Army
Booth became a Methodist minister, but he broke away from the church and began to preach among poor people. In 1878 he created the Salvation Army to fight poverty, drunkenness and crime. William was the first general of the Army, which ran soup kitchens, night shelters and hostels for the poor.

BORGIA, *Lucrezia (1480-1519) Italian noblewoman*
Lucrezia has for centuries been accused of brutal murder, plots and cruelty, but in fact she was innocent of most of these crimes. A beautiful, witty and charming woman, she was forced into 4 political marriages. During her last marriage she spent much of her time doing charitable work among the children of the poor.

BOUDICA, *(c.20-61 AD) Queen of the Iceni*
When the Romans occupied Britain, they behaved
very brutally to Boudica, the widow of the Celtic
king, and her daughters. The Iceni tribe retaliated.
Boudica gathered an army and captured the new
Roman towns of Colchester, St Albans and London,
where her troops slaughtered the inhabitants and
burned the buildings. The Roman governor defeated
her rebel army. Boudica took poison to avoid capture
by the Romans.

BRAILLE, *Louis (1809-1852)*
French inventor of the blind alphabet
Braille was 3 when he went blind. He went to a blind
school in Paris where he learned to read books in
large raised capital letters, and to play the piano.
He became an organist and developed a system of
reading and writing with 6 raised dots to represent
each letter of the alphabet. His alphabet is now used
by blind people all over the world.

BROWN, *John (1800-1859)*
American anti-slavery abolitionist

Brown was violently opposed to slavery and decided the best way to end it was to arm the slaves. He organised a raid to seize the armoury full of rifles and ammunition at Harper's Ferry. Brown expected the slaves to rise in revolt, but a group of marines arrived, killed 15 of his followers and captured him. He was tried for treason and murder, and hanged.

BUTLER, *Josephine (1828-1906) English philanthropist*

Josephine worked in Liverpool helping prostitutes, who were often arrested and imprisoned if they were suspected of carrying disease. People thought it wrong for a woman like Josephine to defend prostitutes, and she was attacked several times. An angry mob even set fire to a hall where she was speaking, but she carried on with her work. Her speeches won the support of many people, and eventually the harsh laws against prostitutes were changed.

C

CADBURY, *George (1839-1922)*
English businessman and social reformer
Cadbury turned his small family firm into a world-famous company for cocoa and chocolate. He also worked to improve the lives of poor people in the cities. He opened a new factory at Bourneville and built a small village of pleasant houses with gardens for his workers. People from all over the world came to study and learn from his experiment.

CARNEGIE, *Andrew (1835-1919)*
Scottish-born American industrialist
Carnegie's family left Scotland when he was 12 and settled in Pittsburgh. They were poor so Carnegie worked in a cotton factory instead of going to school. In his spare time he read as much as he could and saved his money carefully. He started a company building iron bridges, and later began producing steel. Carnegie became very rich, and decided to use his money to help people. He established 2811 free public libraries and gave money to universities in Scotland and the USA.

CAVELL, *Edith (1865-1915) English nurse*
Cavell went to Belgium as a governess, and then trained as a nurse. She became matron of a hospital in Brussels, and during World War I helped many British and French soldiers to escape from the Germans and reach the Dutch frontier. The Germans found out, arrested her, and condemned her to death by firing squad.

CHANEL, *Coco (1883-1971) French fashion designer*
Chanel was an orphan. She designed simple, informal clothes, and introduced her 'little black dress', comfortable jersey dresses, bobbed hair, costume jewellery and her famous perfume, Chanel no. 5.

CHESHIRE, *Leonard (1917-) British Fighter pilot*
Cheshire joined the RAF on the outbreak of World
War II, and won many honours, including the
Victoria Cross. A devout Catholic, he founded the
first Cheshire Home for the Incurably Sick in 1948.
In 1959 he married Sue Ryder who established a
foundation for the sick and disabled of all ages.

COBBETT, *William (1763-1835) English journalist*
Cobbett started a weekly political paper in which he
demanded a better life for the poor. The government
feared that his ideas might incite a revolution.
Cobbett fled to America to avoid further arrest. Back
in England, he toured the country on horse-back and
wrote a book called *Rural Rides* about his journeys.

COLUMBA, *Saint*
(c. 521-597) Irish missionary
Columba became a priest in Ulster and began setting
up churches in Ireland. With a party of 12 followers
he sailed to the island of Iona off Scotland and built
a small monastery. He set out to convert the Picts to
Christianity. He made friends with the local Pict
chief, and converted many
of his warriors. By
the time Columba
died, a large
part of Scotland
became Christian.

DALAI LAMA, *(1935-) Tibetan spiritual leader*
When Tenzin Gyatso was only 2, a group of
Buddhist leaders came to his house seeking the
replacement for the previous Dalai Lama. They
believed the little boy was their new leader, the
Buddha of Compassion come down to Earth. When
he was 4 he was taken to Lhasa (capital of Tibet),
placed on a throne
in a huge palace,
and greeted
with joy by
thousands of
people. When
he was 16
the Chinese
invaded
Tibet. The
Dalai Lama
tried to live
peaceably with
the Chinese,
but 9 years later
had to flee in
disguise across the
Himalayas to India.

DARLING, *Grace (1815-1842) English heroine*
Grace grew up on the Farne Islands in northern
England, where her father was a lighthouse keeper.
One day a paddle steamer was wrecked in a storm.
Most of the people on board were drowned, but
a few managed to scramble onto the rocks. Grace
and her father set off in a rowing boat to rescue
the survivors. After a terrible struggle through
rough seas they reached the rocks and while Grace
looked after the tossing boat, her father lifted the
injured into it. As a result of their bravery 9 people
were rescued.

DAVISON, *Emily (1872-1913) English suffragette*
Emily was a keen supporter of the movement to
give women the right to vote. She joined the
Women's Social and Political Union, and was sent to
prison several times for militant action such as stone
throwing, setting fire to letter boxes, and bombing
the prime minister's country home. She was
trampled to death while trying to stop the king's
horse at the Derby at Epsom.

DIOR, *Christian
(1905-1957)
French fashion designer*
After World War II
there was an immediate
reaction to the dull,
uniform look of
wartime fashions.
Dior became famous
for his 'New Look'
which had softly
rounded shoulders,
small waists and
long swirling skirts.

DUNANT, *Jean Henri (1828-1910)*
Swiss founder of the Red Cross
Dunant helped to tend the wounded at the Battle
of Solferino in 1859, which resulted in 40,000
casualties. He founded the Red Cross in 1864,
but neglected his business affairs and went
bankrupt. He spent the rest of his life in poverty,
but continued to promote the interests of prisoners
of war, the abolition of slavery, and the
establishment of a Jewish homeland.

EDDY, *Mary Baker (1821-1910)*
Founder of the Christian Science movement
From early childhood Mary showed an unusual
interest in religion. She was severely injured in an
accident and was an invalid for many years.
She tried many remedies but did not get any better.
One day after reading in her Bible about one
of Jesus' healings, she decided to try spiritual
healing, and managed to cure herself. She started
the Christian Science movement.

ERASMUS, *Disiderius (c.1466-1536) Dutch scholar*
Erasmus was an orphan brought up in a monastery.
He was exceptionally clever and went to study in
Paris. He visited learned establishments and wrote
many books. He made a new, accurate translation of
the New Testament, and wrote a best-selling book
that poked fun at the worldly, lazy monks.

FOX, *George (1624-1681)*
Founder of the Quaker movement
Fox was disgusted by the wickedness he saw in
the Church of England. He travelled around the
country preaching, and winning support for his
beliefs. He often got into trouble and was
imprisoned 8 times. Once, when on trial, he told the
judge that he should quake before the Lord, so the
judge called him and his followers 'Quakers', as
they have been called ever since.

FRANCIS OF ASSISI, *Saint (1182-1226) Italian friar*
As a young man, Francis had plenty of money and
many friends. He helped his father with his
business, then joined the army. After an illness,
he decided to devote his life to helping the poor. He
gathered round him a number of followers or friars
who dressed in brown cloaks. They vowed to live a
simple life, to obey God and to help the sick and the
poor. They had no possessions and lived by begging
for food.

F

FROEBEL, *Friedrich (1798-1852)*
German educationalist
Froebel was a lonely child who had great difficulty in learning to read. He invented ways to help young children learn through play. He believed that children have a natural pattern of development and that a teacher's task is to help them develop. He established the first kindergarten where the children were encouraged to learn through play, handicrafts and exercise.

FRY, *Elizabeth (1870-1845) English prison reformer*
One day she visited Newgate prison in London and was appalled at the terrible conditions. Many women prisoners had their children in prison with them and were crowded together in dirty, unhealthy cells. Elizabeth set up a school for the children, and trained the women so they could get jobs when they were released.

GANDHI, *Mohandas (1869-1948) Indian leader*
Gandhi was a lawyer who tried to improve the
status of the "Untouchables", the lowest of the
Hindu caste system, and set an example by making
some cloth each day on his spinning wheel.
He became the leader of the National Congress in
their campaign against British rule.
He encouraged his people
to oppose the
government
without using
force. He tried to
heal the divisions
between Hindus
and Moslems, but
was shot and killed
by a Hindu fanatic.

GARIBALDI, *Guiseppi (1807-1882) Italian patriot*
Garibaldi became interested in uniting the separate
states of Italy under a government that would rule
according to the wishes of the people. He took part
in an unsuccessful rebellion and escaped to South
America. He returned to Italy and led 1000 men
wearing red shirts in a revolt in Sicily, then defeated
the King of Naples. When the first all-Italian
parliament was elected, Garibaldi had a seat
representing Rome.

G

GELDOF, *Bob (1954-) Irish rock singer*
Geldof did not do well at school and was often
beaten. He found success with a group called
'The Boomtown Rats'. Geldof decided to help the
starving people of Ethiopia by setting up a charity
called 'Band Aid'. He raised large sums of money
for famine relief by recording the song *'Do they know
it's Christmas?'*. Geldof travelled the world
publicising the problem of famine and asking
famous people to help him. He staged two live pop
charity concerts called 'Live Aid' which were seen
by millions world wide.

GODIVA, *Lady (c.1040-1080)*
Anglo-Saxon gentlewoman
Lady Godiva was so sorry for the poor people of
Coventry that she implored her husband to reduce
their taxes. He said he would only do so if she rode
naked through the crowded market place, which she
did, her long hair covering all her body except her
legs. As a result, her husband freed the town from
all taxes except those on horses.

GOODALL, *Jane (1934-) English zoologist*
Jane decided to go to Africa to see the wildlife.
She met Louis Leakey and became his assistant in
Tanzania. Here she first began to study troops of
chimpanzees and how they make tools. The animals
soon came to accept her and her work showed how
little we know about animals in the wild. She has
written many books and papers on the behaviour
of chimpanzees.

GREGORY, *Saint (c.540-604) Pope*

Gregory was born into a wealthy Roman family, but he longed to become a monk. With a group of friends he turned the family house into a monastery, and together they led a life of prayer and Bible study. Gregory went to Constantinople as the Pope's representative, and on his return to Rome was elected Pope himself. He sent St Augustine to convert the English to Christianity.

HAILE SELASSIE, *(1891-1975) Ethiopian emperor*
Haile Selassie ruled Ethiopia as emperor for more
than 40 years. He spent his time trying to make his
country into a modern state, building hospitals,
factories and schools. But he did not realise that
those he had educated wanted a say in ruling the
country. He was deposed, and his position of
emperor was abolished.

Addis Ababa

GUEVARA, *Che (1928-1967)*
South American revolutionary leader
Guevara was desperately concerned about the
poverty, hunger and disease that he saw among
the people of South and Central America. He tried
to organise revolutions against their oppressors.
He met Castro in Mexico and became one of his
commanders. Together they launched an invasion
of Cuba. Later Guevara took a small force to Bolivia
to organise a revolt among the people. His group
was defeated, Guevara was wounded, captured
and shot.

HARDIE, *James Kier (1856-1915)*
Founder member of the Labour Party
Hardie became a coal miner at 10 years old. He
saw the appalling conditions of the mines and the
injuries or death suffered by the miners in return
for very low wages. He helped organise
miners' unions throughout the
country, and founded the
Scottish Labour Party. He
spoke out in Parliament
against unemployment and
poverty, and supported
votes for women.

SOCIALISM
VOTE
HARDIE

HILL, *Octavia (1838-1912) British social reformer*
At 14 Hill was asked by a charity to run a workshop
where poor children made toy furniture. Later she
ran a school from her own home. She was lent some
money by John Ruskin and bought 3 properties
which she rented to the poor. She tried to get to
know her tenants and to encourage them to pay
their rents on time. Hill was so successful that other
people asked her to manage their properties. She
worked to protect open spaces and provide parks,
and helped found the National Trust.

JACKSON, *Jesse (1941-) American politician*
Jackson was brought up at a time when black and white children in America were not allowed to go to the same schools or eat in the same restaurants. He became a Baptist preacher and worked with Martin Luther King to change the laws that discriminated against black people. Jackson became a leader after King was shot dead and worked to help blacks get better schools and jobs. Although he has never been elected to office, he won almost enough votes to become the Democratic presidential candidate in 1988.

BETTER JOBS
FOR BLACKS

WHITES ONLY
IN THIS
RESTAURANT

JINNAH, *Mohammed Ali (1976-1948) Pakistani leader*
Jinnah trained as a lawyer and on his return to India
became involved in the Indian National Congress.
He worked with Gandhi but came to believe that he
was only interested in the Hindus. Jinna joined the
Muslim League and worked for a separate Muslim
state of Pakistan. Many people died in the riots
between Hindus and Muslims. When Pakistan and
India gained independence, Jinna became Governor-
General of Pakistan, but only lived for another 13
months.

JOHN PAUL II, *Pope (1920-)*
Karol Wojtila was born in Poland. He worked in a
factory during World War II and became a priest
afterwards. He became Poland's youngest bishop
and then a cardinal. When he was elected Pope, he
chose the name of John Paul out of respect to the
previous Pope. He was the first non-Italian pope in
over 450 years. He has made many journeys all over
the world to spread the message of the gospels to
Roman Catholics. He always kisses the ground on
arrival in a country as a sign of love and respect.

KELLER, *Helen (1880-1968)*
American writer and scholar

When Helen was 6 she had a severe illness which left her deaf and blind. She could not make recognisable sounds or make herself understood. Helen learned to read and write in Braille and took a university degree. She spent her life trying to help other people like herself.

KING, *Martin Luther (1929-1968)*
American Black leader

King became a Baptist minister and joined the struggle for black people's rights in America. He led a campaign to end the separation of blacks from whites on public transport and urged his followers not to use violence in their protests. He was often arrested, but gained so much support that 20,000 people joined him in a great civil rights march on Washington. His famous words "I have a dream" inspired millions of people throughout the world to campaign for civil rights. King was shot during a campaign march in Tennessee.

L

LUTHER, *Martin (1483-1546)*
German religious reformer
Luther became a monk after he was nearly killed by a terrible storm. He was a serious person who was worried by his own sins and by the evil in the world. He became the leader of a group of men who thought that the Church had strayed too far from the teachings of the Bible. Luther wrote down all his complaints and nailed them to the church door of Wittenburg cathedral. A fearful argument followed and Luther was expelled from the church. The ruler of Saxony protected Luther who spent the rest of his life teaching and writing. Lutherans formed a new Protestant church.

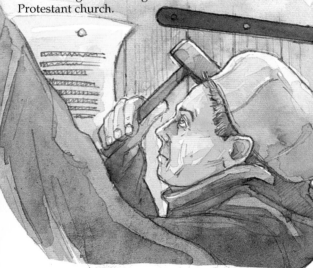

LUTHULI, *Albert (1898-1967) South African politician*
Luthuli was a teacher before he was elected a chieftain of a Zulu tribe in South Africa. He worked for political rights for the blacks. He led peaceful campaigns against the 'apartheid' laws. His auto-biography is called *Let My People Go.*

MALCOLM X , *(1925-1965) American Black leader*
When he was young, Malcolm Little saw his home
burned down by the Klu Klux Klan, a group of
white racists in America. He joined the Black
Muslim organisation. He went on speaking tours
round the country and was not afraid of violence to
achieve his aims. He founded the Organisation of
Afro-American Unity to spread his ideas about
racial solidarity. He was killed at a rally by a
Black Muslim.

MANDELA, *Nelson (1918-) South African politician*
Mandela became active in opposing the 'apartheid'
laws in South Africa . He led a secret organisation
to blow up government property, was arrested and
imprisoned for life. He was set free after many years
because of pressure from people throughout the
world, and led the African National Congress in
their negotiations with the white minority
government to obtain the right to vote
for the blacks. In 1994,
he became President.

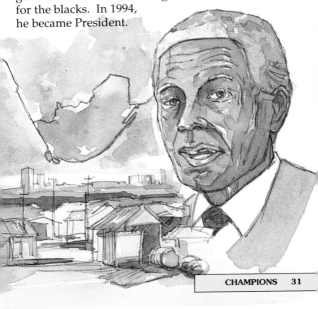

MONTESSORI, *Maria (1870-1852) Italian educationalist*
Montessori was the first Italian woman to study
medicine. She worked with mentally handicapped
children. She developed her own teaching methods
which allowed each child to learn by using the
materials provided in the classroom to solve problems
about the physical world. Later she opened a school
for slum children in Rome. Her methods of teaching
have had a lasting influence on nursery and
infant teaching.

NIGHTINGALE, *Florence (1820-1910) English nurse*
Florence became superintendent of a hospital for sick
women in London, then went with a party of nurses to
the Crimea to take charge of the wounded British
soldiers. On her arrival she worked hard to help the
soldiers and was called the 'lady with the lamp'. She
became a national heroine and on her return to Britain
was given £45,000 which she used to start the
Nightingale Training School for Nurses.

NOBEL, *Alfred (1833-1896) Swedish inventor*
Nobel tried to manufacture a powerful explosive
called nitroglycerin. He blew up his factory by
mistake, killing his brother, but continued his
experiments until he discovered a much safer
explosive which he called 'dynamite'.
His invention made him millions of pounds but
he was sad that his work could cause so much
destruction. When he died, he left most of his
fortune to provide prizes for five scientists, authors,
and workers for peace.

NUFFIELD, *Lord (1877-1963)*
English manufacturer and philanthropist
When William Morris left school, he began to mend
bicycles in a shed near his home. As his business
grew, he started to make bicycles and then to make
Morris cars. His cars were so popular that he made
50,000 a year on a production line, and his factory
gave work to 16,000 people.
Morris was now very rich, and gave his money
freely to research, education and charity.
He established the Nuffield Foundation which gave
money for research into health and education, and
set up the radio telescope at Jodrell Bank.

O

OWEN, *Robert (1771-1858) Welsh social reformer*
Owen owned an important textile mill in Lanark near Glasgow. He was concerned about the welfare of his workers and shortened their working hours, built decent houses for his employees, and opened a school for the children. He believed that if people's working and living conditions improved, their characters would improve too. Owen tried to spread his ideas more widely but people ignored his advice. His greatest influence was upon a small group of workers who began the first co-operative society.

PANKHURST, *Emmeline (1858-1928)*
English suffragette

Emmeline and her husband campaigned to win women the right to vote. When he died, she and her daughter Christabel founded the Women's Social and Political Union, the 'suffragettes'. They chained themselves to railings, interrupted meetings with their slogans, and smashed shop windows. They were frequently arrested and imprisoned, where they went on hunger strikes and had to be force fed. Their campaign was successful and women were eventually given the vote.

GIVE WOMEN THE RIGHT TO VOTE

PARNELL, *Charles Stewart (1846-1891) Irish politician*
Parnell believed the Irish should have their own
government. He led the Home Rule movement in
Parliament and held up debates by making long
speeches. Parnell as President of the Land League
backed the poor Irish farmers who refused to pay
rent. He was put in prison but the government had
to release him to stop the riots and violence which
broke out. Eventually Gladstone agreed Ireland
should have Home Rule.

PERON, *Eva (1919-1952) Argentine politician*
Eva was born into a poor family. She started acting
when she was 15. She became well known on radio
and met Colonel Peron, who became President of
Argentina. Eva encouraged the poor, whom she
called the 'Shirtless Ones', to support her husband.
She organised the women and got them the vote.
She gave food, money
and medicine to the
needy and helped
to promote better
hospitals and
housing. She died
of cancer aged 33.

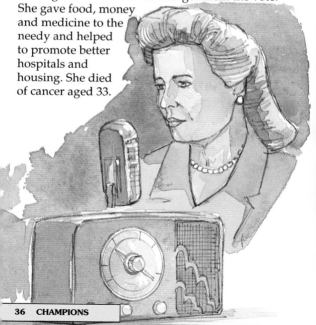

PESTALOZZI, *Johan (1746-1827) Swiss educationalist*
Pestalozzi opened a school for poor children and
taught them spinning and weaving. He developed
a theory that children learned by natural
development, and that teaching should proceed
from the familiar to the unknown. He stressed
the importance of mother and home in a child's
education. His methods became widely accepted
and have been absorbed into modern teaching
techniques.

PLATO, *(c.427-c.347 BC) Greek philosopher*
Plato studied under Socrates and wrote down their
discussions. After Socrates' death Plato founded his
own school of philosophy. He believed that the right
way to teach was to ask questions and let the pupils
discover the truth for themselves. His school, the
Academy on the outskirts
of Athens, lasted for
800 years.

ROOSEVELT, *Eleanor (1884-1962)*
American social reformer

Eleanor married Franklin D. Roosevelt before he became President of the USA. When Roosevelt became ill from polio, she became "the legs and eyes of a crippled husband." She helped and supported him and visited mines, slums and hospitals where he could not go himself. Eleanor always spoke up for the poor, blacks and women and continued to make speeches and write articles for newspapers even after her husband died.

SAUNDERS, *Dame Cicely (1918-)*
English philanthropist

Cicely was working in a hospital as a medical social worker when she became friends with a dying Polish patient. They discussed the idea of hospices which would provide comfortable, caring environments for the dying. When her patient died, he left her £500 to start her off. She trained as a doctor, then began research into the control of pain for the dying. She opened the first hospice in 1967.

SCHWEITZER, *Albert (1875-1965)*
French medical missionary

Schweitzer was a leading scholar and famous organist. He gave everything up to become a mission doctor in Africa. He built a hospital with his own hands at Lambarene. He raised money by giving concerts in Europe. He spent the rest of his life enlarging his hospital and the nearby leper colony and caring for the sick.

SCOTT, *Sir Peter (1909-1989) British naturalist*
Scott was one of the first people to warn the world
of the dangers to the environment caused by
pollution. He was particularly interested in birds
and founded a Wildfowl Trust as a refuge for
waterfowl from all over the world. Later he founded
the World Wildlife Fund, and invented the Red Data
Books for framing international laws on
conservation. He painted pictures of birds, wrote,
and broadcast on the natural world.

SEACOLE, *Mary (1805-1881) Jamaican nurse*
When Mary heard about the Crimea War, she
longed to join Florence Nightingale. She travelled to
England and asked permission to go as a nurse, but
was refused because she was coloured. Mary took a
boat to the Crimea at her own expense, and on
arrival built a store and a kitchen near the front line.
Every day she took food and medicine to the
soldiers, bandaged the wounded and gave comfort
to the dying. Back in England after the war, grateful
soldiers gave her money to save her from poverty.

SHAFTESBURY, *7th Earl of (1801-1885)*
English social reformer

Shaftesbury persuaded Parliament to pass laws to stop children working in textile mills or in coal mines, to ban boys working as chimney sweeps, and to reduce the hours of factory workers. He set up 'ragged schools' for very poor children, ran soup kitchens for the hungry, and improved the conditions for the mentally handicapped. The statue of Eros was erected in Piccadilly Circus, London, in his memory.

SOCRATES, *(c.470-c.400 BC) Greek philosopher*

Socrates was an original thinker. He developed a method of teaching by asking questions, and was the first to use a set of rules, or logic, to discuss important matters. He was always searching for the truth and wanted to make the complex problems of life easier to understand. His enemies tried him for corrupting the young, and he was sentenced to death by drinking a deadly poison.

SOLOMON, *King (962-922 BC) Hebrew king*

Solomon was a wise and just king. He was a good commander, but preferred to make friends of his enemies. He introduced taxation reforms which relieved the poorer parts of his country, encouraged trade and the mining industry, and made his country rich. He built the first Jewish temple in Jerusalem, and people came from far and wide to visit him and see the beautiful things he had in his palace.

STONE, *Lucy (1818-1893) American suffragette*

Lucy's father refused to send her to school because he saw no value in educating women. She joined an anti-slavery society which also allowed her to speak on women's rights. She gained wide publicity when she refused to take her husband's name after marriage. She helped to establish the American Woman Suffrage Association and edited the Woman's Journal, a paper which defended women's rights to vote.

STOPES, *Marie (1880-1958) Pioneer of birth control*
Marie Stopes had a very unhappy first marriage
and separated from her husband. At that time it
was thought wrong to talk about sexual matters,
but Marie wrote two books that clearly explained
sex, birth control and family planning.
Many people were shocked but others wrote to
thank Marie and ask for more information. After her
second marriage, Marie opened a family planning
clinic in London. Her work meant people could talk
more openly about sex.

T

TERESA, *Mother (1910-) Yugoslav nun*

When she became a nun, sister Teresa went to India to teach in a wealthy girl's school in Calcutta. One day she felt that God wanted her to help the poor by living and working among them. She got permission to leave the convent, changed her nun's habit for a sari, and went to the poorest parts of Calcutta. She found 5 destitute children and sheltered them in a friend's flat. As the numbers grew, she established a new order of nuns, the Missionaries of Charity. They cared for orphans, the dying, the blind, aged and crippled. She later established a leper colony. There are now Missionaries for Charity caring for the poor in many parts of the world.

TONE, *Wolfe (1763-1798) Irish patriot*

Wolfe Tone wanted to free Ireland of English rule.
He organised rebel groups, and founded the Society
of United Irishmen to unite Catholics and
Protestants in a bid for independence.
He went to France to get support for a
revolutionary uprising backed by French troops.
When he landed in Ireland his group was defeated.
Tone was captured and tried, but committed suicide
in prison before he could be hanged for treason.

TUBMAN, *Harriet (c.1820-1913) American abolitionist*

Harriet was a slave in Maryland, USA, who escaped
to the North by the Underground Railway, an
escape system for fugitive slaves run by people who
wanted to abolish slavery. The next year she
returned to Maryland to help guide
members of her family in their escape. For 10 years
she was one of the most active guides on the
Underground Railway, and helped over 300 slaves
escape. She became known as the 'Moses of her
people' for helping lead so many slaves to freedom.

TUTU, *Desmond (1931-) South African archbishop*
When Tutu became a priest he decided to oppose the
policy of 'apartheid' in South Africa. As Dean of
Johannesburg he could have lived in a pleasant white
area, but chose to live in Soweto, a crowded township
for a million black people. He became Archbishop of
Capetown and has been given many honours for
speaking out for black people.

TYLER, *Wat (d.1381) English rebel leader*
When the king decided to impose more taxes on
the peasants Tyler led a ragged army of peasants to
London in protest. In London the rebels presented a
petition to King Richard to demand lower rents and
an end to their oppression at work. The young king
agreed, but at a later meeting, Tyler was badly
wounded and later beheaded on the orders of the
Mayor of London.

WESLEY, *John (1703-1791)*
English founder of Methodism

Wesley became a priest and with his brother Charles formed a group nicknamed the 'methodists' who met together to pray and read the Bible. One day Wesley attended a gospel meeting in London that changed his life. He felt he had been given a sign of God's love . He travelled all over England holding services and preaching. He organised 'methodist' societies with ordinary people as preachers, and his movement gradually grew away from the Church of England.

WILBERFORCE, *William (1759-1833)*
English reformer

Wilberforce became a Member of Parliament and spent his whole life campaigning for the abolition of slavery. Parliament finally passed a law to stop the slave trade, but employers in the West Indies still wanted slaves and the trade continued secretly. Wilberforce decided the only way was to stop people from owning slaves at all, and after another long campaign the law was passed.

WYCLIFFE, *John (c.1320-1384)*
English religious reformer

Wycliffe attacked the Catholic Church saying that the priests were too wealthy and corrupt. He believed that no man had the right to own property if he was a sinner and that the king had the right to take away the property of the Church if the priests did not do their duty. To help his followers, he encouraged the first translation of the Bible from Latin into English. Because he encouraged people to pray directly to God, he was condemned as a dangerous heretic and his writings were publicly burnt.